I0117215

Stupid Mind

When Curse Becomes Blessing

Som Gurung

chipmunkapublishing
the mental health publisher

Som Gurung

Published by
Chipmunkapublishing
United Kingdom

http://www.chipmunkapublishing.com

Copyright © 2016 Som Gurung

ISBN   978-1-78382-161-7

We live in a multi-ethnic society with different cultures, values and festivals. We welcome various vibrant trends and embrace traditions that we are accustomed to. The communities that we belong to are constantly evolving and becoming more and more diverse. We tend to learn, accept, and appreciate the multiculturalism around us with the progression of such changes.

I feel lucky to live amongst people who are open-minded. I feel privileged to be living in a society where I am free to speak my mind, where I am protected by the government, where I can enjoy my human rights without any fear, where I have been given freedom to choose what I believe and what religion I want to follow without the fear of discrimination. I feel immensely fortunate for where I am today and what I am able to accomplish.

However, something that never fails to surprise me in our modern and advanced society, where civilization has developed so much, where humans have become sophisticated beyond imagination, is that still in this day and age we find people who are called names like weirdo, mental etc. That some people are still labelled by members of our society because they are different in the way that they feel, the way in which they chose to live their lives and how they think. This is often done without any realisation of the impact these kinds of attitudes have on people's lives.

I often hear 'normal' people talk about vulnerable people with mental health issues in a patronizing and derogatory manner, discriminating against them. These people who need support and care to fight with their 'darker sides' are often neglected and often mistreated.

Many people suffering with mental health issues have been through very rough times and suffered traumas. Many of them have been through things in their lives, which have led them to lose their hopes and aspirations.

I want you to imagine that your world is suddenly turned upside down, that your hopes, your dreams and your aspirations are shattering before your eyes. How would you react? Would you cry and scream for months on end? Perhaps even longer, until you are finally able to recover, to find hope and the courage to put your life back together.

But what if time fails to heal you? What if you are not able to embrace life as normally as other people do, as you once did.

How then will you fight? How will you learn to live when you feel life caving in around you; when you feel like giving up every day, every second?

These are just some of the issues that many with mental health issues face on a monthly, weekly and even daily basis.

Yet, regardless of the stigma from our society, I have experienced amongst these 'abnormal' people, some of the most amazing characteristics; the highest creativity and the greatest level of humanity. I have witnessed more so than in any other places, their simplicity, their courage in dealing with daily mental and physical sufferings, their desire to be loved by their friends and family, their wish to live life without being depressed, to have joy and most importantly to be treated with love and respect like everyone else.

Stupid Mind reflects the period of my life when I was experiencing episodes of abnormality, when I was often criticized by the people close to me. It reflects my darker side, which at times was disturbing and unsettling.

But it also reflects the brighter side of the psychological dysfunction that I experienced; a side which has actively allowed me to create the person that I am today, and has thus provided me with a wealth of new insights, courage and strength. Through these insights, I now realise that this experience would not be possible without the curse of the illness that fostered it.

Once a wise man said that "to live is the rarest thing in the world, most people just exist." This is quite true in today's world, where many people have forgotten how to live. The quicker I accept the fact that my Time is limited, the quicker I will learn not to regret any moment in my life and pursue my real happiness.

For this reason, I proudly share my feelings, thoughts, experiences, my fantasies and my opinions without the fear of people judging me once again. From my experience of being labelled and judged by society, I can know that it is immensely difficult to try and live a normal life, to be confident, and to believe in yourself, when most of the people around you do not take you seriously. And yet I give you these very private poems and stories. I give them to you regardless of the fact that I do not know who you are or where you are coming from. I do not know whether you will take them seriously or decide to ridicule me after reading them, but still I give them to you unreservedly - as my gift.

Som Gurung

"Whoever revealed to us the essence of the world would disappoint us almost unpleasantly. It is not the world as a thing in itself, but the world as idea (an error) that is so rich in meaning, deep, wonderful, pregnant with happiness and unhappiness." Fredrick Nietzsche

WELCOME TO MY LIFE

They decided to lock me up again, they said I was paranoid
They said hearing voices was taboo
The invisible giggles
Screams that made me terrified
Those shrill voices
Those melodious whispers
Those intimate laughers
Deep in my ear
Those strangers who laughed hysterically
And those who screamed in terror

Again those pills came to subdue
Then lights got dimmer
Eyes got blurry
Heart started to sink; seized tremor

Last night a giant hawk came to visit me
Flapping her mighty ferocious wings
She woke me from unconsciousness
Panicked me; powerless surrender

She could be the messenger
Eccentric creed
Warm air from each beat cursing my face
Scary indeed

You decided that you will not meet me anymore
And I knew I could never see you again
Slowly I forgot your name
And then I forgot your face
I do not know what happened to you anymore
And for a long time you have been dead

When you decided that I was a risk to you
I knew I would never hear from you again
Memories started eroding
Slowly I forgot your smiles
Slowly I forgot to cry
And for a long time I have seen gloom

TRING!! TRING!! The phone rang
I was scared and angry
I picked up and screamed this time
"RIGHT I HAVE LEARNED MY FUCKING LESSON?
How can I be so confused when you are not even real?"
The voice on the other side whispered wistfully
"What the hell are you talking about?"
Then soon faded away
I was confused as hell

But if I could chose
I would chose sweet dreams over disturbing nightmares
I would chose to wake up each day feeling fresh
I would chose to feel the eternal happiness
I would chose to step out in the sunlight
And I would then smile truly
And under the blue sky I would sink deeply

But what can I do
You have decided that I am just impulsive
Critical and demanding
You have decided that I will never change
So there is no point in pretending
But if I do so
Can I ask you to not pretend as well?
Coz when you look me in the eyes directly
I know why you are grinning

They say I struggle with outright psychosis
I live in delusion
Common syndrome
Bipolar depression
But who would chose the devil if they knew?
It's not what I wished out of the blue

Som Gurung

They say action is powerful, I say words are powerful
Words can create histories; words can burn them down
again
I am stupid!! But where would you find a survivor like me
Only in darkness if you can see

If you swim deep you will find the real gems
Along the shallow water you can only find pebbles
Sometimes my stupid mind and I discuss thoughts
My senseless mind argues with me, I think its nuts

She thinks I am deep and thoughtful
She does not know I will be destroyed eventually
But while I am still here
Like a burning candle
Let me shine through the darkness around me

"Our crime against criminal is we treat them like scoundrels"
Fredrick Nietzsche

DREAM

If I had wings I would fly
To the far, far paradise
Where people love each other
Where people care for each other

If I had wings I would fly
Somewhere
Where all fears disappear
No more hunger
No more greed
Serenity prevails

If I could chose to see
I would only see
The colours of love
If I could chose to hear
I would chose
The only voice of truth
In the wilderness of dense forest
In the mist of rain

If I had wings I would fly
Where everyone celebrates one festival
I would fly to rejoice
Where all the dreamers are

"*So much like the state-dependent memories in dreams in which the landscapes errie familiarity reminds you that you've visited the identical locale before in other dreams. Same with marijuana-a couple of hits and suddenly you're in a familiar place thinking familiar thoughts that exist only in the marijuana state. "Irvin Yalom*

OLD HEALER

I dream about the place lying in high mountains
Higher than the highest, risky and dangerous terrain
Where dense fog carpets the landscape mostly
Where they lay in the silky brusqueness
Where the rays are often dim
Where rain is so cold and soothing
See through the eyes of the dreamer
It's such a golden bless

If you stay till late
In that paradise
When the sun changes colour again
And hides slowly behind the mountain
When birds start to chirp again
Singing and dancing in golden bliss
You will see an infinity of fireflies illuminate the sky
And you transpire into a different world again
I close my eyes
And I see heaven
Somewhere in this world is that place
Where silent mother peacefully breathes

And close by there is a meadow
I can see some human locomotion
A bunch of people
Young, old and children
Their face shines
And in front of them is an old healer

Stupid Mind

The old healer looks so fragile
But his face glows of love and kindness
And only he can heal my wounds
Something tells me that he can cure my illness

But lord I have sinned
And heaven does not belong to me
I am desperate
But I have no ticket to that place

"We love life, not because we are used to living but because we are used to loving" Fredrick Nietzsche

HEART- BREAK

A troubled man never was at such peace
His face was numb in the passing breeze
Slowly as he exhaled again the long breath
I wondered how that pain will ever ease

Sitting next to him she laid
Such a young lady with a pretty face
She rests her soft cheek over his lap
And her tears roll silently
She the heaven's child
Cannot see him take this flight

He is sitting in his wheel chair
He is gazing away from her
Hoping someday they will reunite
Hoping someday they will fly together
He tries to hide
But his tears keep rolling
He the daring warrior
Now a man who fears

And once again I was there
Watching hopelessly
From the distant
Under the sycamore tree
And around me field of barley
I did not move until his soul finally departed
Leaving the loving wife
His soul left the sight

The wild roses and rhododendron
In the forest are still blooming
Wild River still washes the shore
Still fiercely flowing
But there is a barren and isolation
In the little house within the mist of a tiny field

Summer came but said nothing
Neither did winter, autumn and spring
All those memories; now just a memory lane

Gone but never forgotten; sweet reveries
Swallowed by the fate; the warm melodies
Only remain now; the feeling of emptiness
And the gift that follows; constant sullenness
And all those memories, those delights, the cheerfulness
The happiness of lovers
You can see in the wistful silence

For the last time, I visited the house again
I stood in the same spot
And watched from a distance
When the sun rose again
She was lying in his wheel chair
But her soul had drifted and taken a flight
In memory, I bowed my head
And said a final goodbye
To the dreamers of wonderland

"He is civilized, polite, a man of manners. He has tamed his wild nature, turned his wolf into a spaniel. And he calls this moderation. Its real name is mediocrity. "Fredrick Nietzsche

STUPID MIND

Hey! I've got to tell you something
Will you listen to me?
Ah! After you listen to me
Don't forget to appreciate
Ok! Higher power is high
And stupid mind is creating something
It's wrong
No it's right
It's Michael Jackson's black or White
Oh, sorry to confuse you, man
I promise I won't do it again
Ah ha - I am just kidding!
OK!! Stupid mind wonders why people fall in love
If they have to breakup
Why isn't there such thing as happy ever ending
Tears roll from eyes
And tears dry
Love is passion
Love hurts! Why?
But I still say it's a beautiful world
And I guess money can buy everything
Ok, now I am being stupid
But hey, stupid mind understands science and technology
Oh! Stupid mind is busy

Oh! Stupid mind is busy
Writing some stuff
Stupid mind can't understand what
And stupid mind can't understand why
So why don't you become my friend
And teach me the right things?
And tell me if I am wrong
Coz I might be wrong
And, my friend
If I am too wrong

Pull the trigger
Do not hesitate to fire the gun
Coz it's worse for me to be ashamed
Than bleed to death

Does it make sense, what I have said?
Or am I just being a nuisance?
Oh! Have I confused you yet again?
Oh! Sorry, sir and madam
If I have
Maybe I will leave you alone
Ah ha - I am just kidding

Hey! Do you know, most of the time I just fight!
To preserve the last of my sanity
Other times I write
So that I can be proud of my insanity
So that I can tell you my story
In a different light, in a different glory

"Indeed I have often laughed at the weaklings who think themselves good merely because they have lame paws."
Fredrick Nietzsche

SPIRIT

It's a stormy evening
The sky is thundering and lightning strikes
It's filled with dark and angry clouds
A Strong wind is blowing
Heavy rain, and altogether
The whole village is blazing
There is passion
There is a call for rebellion
The farmers are sharpening their metals
The victims are ready for war
Everyone is alive
And everyone is vigilant

I was living my life in fantasy
I was living without meaning
Trapped in filthy thoughts
Travelling to messy places
Until this traveller came to a tiny village
Where he found the new meaning to existence
A new kind of sensation
Like the way it grows
Now I am ready to follow
Wherever it goes

These people are more alert
Fighting for revolution
They said they ran from brutality
But there is no more hiding place
They say that they've had enough now
Now they want difference

They are ready for battle
They are prepared to die
This is not an ordinary day
After being oppressed
And after being tortured for so long
Sufferers have learned to self-defend

They are no more innocent and harmless
They are ready to kill or be killed

Now the merciless demons
Who used to destroy innocent lives
Will feel the fear too
These demons are trapped in their own device
This time they will figure out
The odour of these new executioners
Come forth from the atrocities
Waiting to avenge those innocent lives
These dictators will know how mad people are
And that their victims are powerless no more

As I was joining their revolt in ore
One of them looked me in the eyes
And said
This is going to be disturbing
Oh, noble visitor, I appreciate your assistance
But how can you be involved?
You are not part of it
Thinking is something
And doing is something different
When you break and get crushed
The pain is excruciating

Then he said again:
*I am doing this for my brothers, sisters, children and our
future generation*
For them, I am ready to go through this new beginning

The start of insanity
Leave as soon as you can
Unless you are connected to the common spirit
You don't have reason to be a part of it

Then I said:
I have never seen this way of living
I really want to feel it
You are richer then the filthy millionaires
Filled with reason and passion
Electrifies every single bone in me

Once Nietzsche said:
If we climb high enough tragedy ceases to look tragic
And I guess if tragedy is no more a tragedy it is enlightenment
It's a transition into higher level of peace and serenity
When you have clearer vision you are always in a better place

"If you have an enemy, do not repay his evil with good: for that would put him to shame, But rather prove that he has done something good to you." Fredrick Nietzsche

MESSAGE TO ENEMY

Gained more panic attacks from fantasies than real occurrences
Listening to your bullshit makes my hopes turn to despair
Nowadays I cringe with fingers in my ears when you speak
And all the words you mumble don't make me care

But enemies are a common teacher, we should learn from them
They try to prolong my misery, profit from the situation
Seeking to turn my misfortune into their advantage
This, my friend, is known as secondary gain

So here is what I really have to say!
If you are so prepared to hear me, brace yourself
Before I do the more sensible thing
Part away and proceed in my own vein

And about your completely false opinion
Here is what I have to say
"Thank you very much for giving voice to your opposition
And giving me this opportunity to listen"
"I am aware this is what you wanted to hear
I hope I made you glisten."
I do not believe a single word you have to say
And I really don't care so have a nice day

"Dissect your motives deeper! No one has ever done anything wholly for others. All actions are self directed, all service is self-serving, and all love is self loving. Perhaps you think of those whom you love, think deeper, and you will learn you do not love them: what you love is a pleasant sensation such love produces in you! You love desire, not the desired." Irvin Yalom

BEWARE

Let me show you the way to heaven where happiness lives eternally
Where all your sorrows and all your pain will disappear eventually
Where you will never hunger for anything
Let me show you the way to heaven's gate
But beware!
It's filled with a thousand traps and a million snares
And deceiving fruits that look delicious
It's filled with venomous poisons
And the prices you have to pay
Strange fantasies; emotional turbulence

Beware that the wild honey grows in the highest mountains
And that this nectar belong to hives of bees
Beware the mesmerising flowers that grow in the deepest forests
They belong to a kingdom of wolves and tigers

Beware if you are infected
Beware you are the carrier of ugly sperm
Be aware if you are a visitor from the city of the selfish
The loyal soldiers of heaven will fight you till their last breath

"The demand to be loved is the greatest kind of arrogance."
Fredrick Nietzsche

BLACK MAGIC WOMAN

She's a black magic woman
She's got me hypnotized
She's poisoned my blood
Now she's running through my vein

She is such a drama queen
Those bloody, moist lips
Those eyes layered in delicate liner
Coveted beneath red silky hair

She likes rolling in the big city
Like a roller coaster
I go crazy when she walks
She's like a 90's Mercedes
She likes blazing that purple haze
She is a nut cracker
Hate the way she smiles
Hate the way she stares
I am crying my heart out
While she's flying in the air

She is a storm in the highway
Burning all desires
Hate the way she talks
Hate the way she walks
Rocking them denim leather
She's a fucking heart breaker

Som Gurung

"Seen from the standpoint of youth, life is an endlessly long future; from that of old age it resembles a very brief past."
Arthur Schopenhauer

HEALING GRACE

Oh, what wonderful weather lately
Fleeting clouds in deep blue sky, like white cotton candy
Chirping birds hiding in nests beneath the bushes
Weaver's tweeters!
Bless the surviving trees
For they have survived storms and rains of yesterdays
Such a glorious day
Here comes the healing grace

Little soldiers hand in hand
Run around the green battle field
Smile brightly! Show your white teeth, milky
Grin once more bright and clearly
New lovers! Underneath the old oak tree, kissing
passionately
These little things, believe me, they are priceless
Little smiles, little moments; Heaven's bliss

Hopes and dreams, they fought fiercely with the winds of
darkness
Now giving way to summertime
Hello sunshine! Wake me up now
So I can dance brightly
Though yesterday was cold and wet;
Indeed shivery
Screaming trees, crying clouds
You have fought the battle well
And you deserve the celebration,
Cheers to victory

Stupid Mind

Before the cold rain lurks from the dark
And everyone disappears
Let's forget the pain of yesterdays
Enjoy the gift of golden rays
Let's make the most of this happy gallantry

"Most politician and business people are clever, very few are intelligent. Whatever is attained through cleverness is short lived and turns out eventually to be self-defeating. Cleverness divides; intelligence includes." Ekhart Tolle

POLITICIAN

Mr Politician!
The more you talk, the more I feel like you are playing mind games
My hopes are turning into despair
Even law is biased here
It does not serve the underclass and poor
Mr Politician!
The rich are only getting richer
Poor are poorer

Mr Politician!
I believe in diversity
I believe that it's the future
But I don't believe in simple solutions
When there is so much segregation
I am happy that I have democracy to live under
I hope you can harness this creation
And I will clap my hands when you give speeches
And I shall always remain sincere
So that I can be proud of this world
And be a humble citizen

I will clap my hands sincerely
While you take your bows
If you can provide a community
Where for real problems there are real solutions
You are the chosen ones
With power comes responsibility
And you will truly deserve the authority
If you can learn to listen to everyone

"No human can always achieve, always create. No human being can be continuously successful in his endeavours. But to go in the right direction, not to have achieved, but achieving, not arriving at the inn but walking towards the inn, not resting on the laurels, putting one's talents to the most constructive, productive, and creative use-this is perhaps the main sense of life and the only possible answer to the existential neurosis which cripples human efforts and maims human mind." Irvin Yalom

INSPIRATION

When climbing high mountains, when walking through tough roads
My friend! If you believe in yourself then you should carry on
Even when all your friends leave you behind!

When people betray your faith and trust
When you feel weak after hitting rock bottom
If people laugh at you!
Let them have orgasms
It's not easy my friend but carry on

After every storm there is a brighter day
After every thunder there is beautiful ray
Like the metal iron that burns for hours
You too will easily mould and evolve anew
You too will become strong today

No one can break and scatter you
If you believe in the strength inside you
I have said and I have done
Ignore me if you think I am wrong
But if you carry on
Abracadabra! Thou shall be blessed

"We like to be out in nature so much because it has no opinion about us." Fredrick Nietzsche

RAINY DAY IN THE WONDERLAND

After flying in a boundless sky for long hours
The tired sun finally yawned
It's time to creep behind those mountains
It's time to sleep
Then the moon appeared slowly
Softly piercing the dark sphere
The mysterious night gently awakened
Tenderly whispered in my ears

Ahhhh!
Now I understand why you went so crazy for her
Oh such amazing wonder
She is so beautiful
The way she looks in that glowing silk
She can illuminate the night sky brighter than the moon
When she comes and dances
Even nightmares are surreal

Tired sun finally yawned
At last, time to creep behind the mountains
The shining moon appeared slowly, piercing the dark sphere
The mysterious night gently whispered into my ear

I whispered back to the night

Hush
Everyone thinks I am crazy
My friends have given up on me lately
These days I am always drunk
And sometimes stumble on my relatives' yard
Tell them they can berate me
Tell them they can tell me to go away
Tell them they can say whatever they wish

Stupid Mind

Tell them I know that I have never been good
So when I am gone, they can rejoice
I have never been good to them
So they can rejoice when I am gone

I whispered back to the night again

But don't tell them that I still miss her
And her memories
And those moments
That I spent with her
Coz they will laugh at me
They will never understand

After ruminating and drinking the night away
I stagger aimlessly
The morning rays kiss the earth again
It's been a while since I have been happy

Every sip I take from the bottle, takes me closer
Every time I lose control ... I feel nearer to the wonderland

"The final reward of the dead is to die no more." Fredrick
Nietzsche

ANOTHER FUCKING PHASE

Some drops make an ocean
Some drops make rain,
Some drops from the vein
On the floor
Some people fly…
To feel pain no more
How beautiful
If some shallow coffin finds me in July

I ask the wolves running wild
Will they teach me how to fly?
So that I can feel the essence
Running from my finger tip
Deep into my soul

Then maybe I will find courage
To dive into the deep water
Then maybe I don't have to ask my destiny
Or swim back to the shore
Then maybe I will not be scared of my vision
And then maybe I will find my salvation
Crazy thoughts
…
Just another fucking phase

"Politically, in symbolic constitutional structures symbolic representatives indicate the will of the people as expressed in symbolic votes; almost no one anymore understands what it means to exert political initiative or come to a communal agreement. Emotionally, a few artists catch from real experience symbols of passion and sensory excitement; these symbols are abstracted and stereotyped by commercial imitators; and people make love and adventure according to these norms of glamour. Medical scientists and social workers provide other symbols of emotion and security, and people make love, enjoy recreation, and so forth according to prescription. "Paul Goodman

YOU CAN FOLLOW SINCERELY

Fiery sun finally dies
Beautiful diamonds! Time to rise
Memories! Reminiscing through nights
Moon and stars! Shine a million lights
You can speak softly
You can sit quietly
Underneath the gloomy tree
Stars shine clearly
And if you're a dreamer
You can follow sincerely

Beneath the shinning paradise
You will find a love to more than suffice
And when it rains
Blessed and tranquil is the occasion
Friends tell me "He is crazy"
But I find them stupid
For my soul so seized
Is now painted in blue

Time after time I survived bravely
Those days were innocent
Yet I was so frenzied

Wounds heal as time flies by
A lullaby to sing through lonely nights
If the gloomy sky thunders
You can drink heavily
And when it rains
You can weep silently
Through wet eyes
Passion shines clearly
And if you can see it
You can follow sincerely

"I only write from my own experience. I write in blood, and the best truth is a bloody truth" - Fredrick Nietzsche

LOST

Don't ask me where I am today
I will just lie to you
Don't ask me if I am happy
Don't make me lie again
I have tried so many years
Still I don't know where I belong
I have tried so many years
But I am still suffocating
How can I breathe?
Don't ask me
These days, I have even forgotten to lie

"*Humans suffered more at the hands of each other than through any natural disasters. By the year 1914, however, the highly intelligent human mind has invented not only internal combustion engine, but also bombs, machine guns, submarines, flame thrower and poisonous gas, Intelligence in the service of madness*" Eckhart Tolle

DARKNESS

It's worse than any other disaster
When not only mind but also heart bleeds in service of craziness
Thoughts are wild; they go insane sometimes but can't stop nevertheless
Sometimes they make you feel paranoid and see the things that are not real
But I am beginning to like it; I guess I am obsessed

I am a dreamer who is dreaming
You won't see my wound and how I am bleeding
People are too clever these days
Obsessed with others' drama and crises
So when I talk
They take interest

You know the trend that's popular?
People hurting each other, inflicting pain and horror
Obsessed with power
Fanatics and murders
Running the race
Stepping over each other
If you don't know this part of civilization yet
Evil of the planet earth belonging to the human race
Then I must say you are truly blind
Then I must say you are truly naïve

So open your eyes and look around
Be sound and focused
Coz you can easily be the next one
Waiting to be abused

"Often the individual desires someone whom the reason tells him to avoid, but the voices of reason is impotent against the forces of sexual passion" the Schopenhauer cure – Irvin Yalom

OBESSSION

I am scared, I am running
I am a lion but she is cunning
I try so hard
But she is always one step behind
With that beauty and charm, always trying
I guess she will never stop chasing

But still I try hard
Though she runs through my head
Sometimes she giggles so loud in my dreams
It makes me wake up in the middle of night
But when I open my eyes
And don't see her pretty face
Joy turns into despair
Coz she comes into dreams, but never for real
Oh, my sex goddess
I don't want to be your desperate lover
So please stop chasing me
But even when I close all my boundaries
She still gets to me!

Som Gurung

"The ultimate evil is that Time is perpetual perishing and being actually involves elimination" Irvin Yalom

CEMETRY

Storm came fiercely
Followed by the gushing wind
I visited the cemetery today
To see tombstones lying
The grasses has gone wild again
Posh graves with classy marbles
In this rain
I hope they feel colder
Or are they just dust
Sleeping; unconcerned

The place was long deserted
There are now wild bushes
Dried sycamore leaves
Drenched in rain
Don't know if I will be here in summer again
I feel the soak under my shoes
As I sit in a rusty metal chair
Sloppy landscape
Memories here and there

And from the long pine trees come birds
Prying at this visitor
Beneath the elegant maple trees
Still withering
The cemetery lies on a tiny hill
Although the storm has stopped
Here the wind is cold; never still

The coldness numbs my face
And the icy air feels sharp in my ear
In the sky, the clouds grow darker by the hour
Looks as if it is again going to shower

In this village of dead
Why have I come here today?
Surely I did not come for answers
But I am searching here and there
I am looking at those dead names carved in stones
Memories forever
Some were too young, some were older
And looking for an answer
The answer to life?
And the answer was death?
End of stories
Buried under

"Sal, thirty-year-old patient, who had developed multiple myeloma, a painful disabling form of bone cancer, toured high schools in the area, counselling teenagers on the hazards of drug abuse and used his cancer and his visibly deteriorating body as a powerful leverage in his mission. The whole auditorium trembled when Sal in a wheelchair, frozen in his cast, exhorted: "you want to destroy your body with nicotine or alcohol or heroine? You want to smash it up in autos? You're depressed and jump off a bridge? Then give me your body! Let me have it! I want it! I'll take it! I want to live!" Irvin Yalom

CHANGE

Lately, I am feeling differently
I don't miss those crazy friends; the night parade
Loud music, disco lights, whiskies and wines
Tipsy legs, shaking eardrums and the wild vibes

I was always scared to be alone, I never wanted to be
But I desired to be valiant; more independent

I had to learn new ways
And face lonely nights
I tried to find answers
Thoughts constant

Eventually I learned different ways
Tough roads were ahead but I carried on
Gloomy thoughts, but this time I didn't let them intimidate
And when I heard my inner voice, I rejoiced

I don't have to fear people and their opinion
These days are easy; strong head and clear mind
Creating new dreams, aims and aspirations
And, under this new grace, life is more assured and fun

"When walking around the top of an abyss, or crossing a deep stream on the plank, we need a railing not to hold onto (for it would collapse with us at once), but rather to achieve the visual image of security. Likewise, when we are young, we need people who unconsciously offer us the service of that railing; it is true that they would not help us if we really were in great danger and wanted to lean on them; but they give us the comforting sensation of protection nearby (for example, fathers, teachers, friends, as we generally know all three)" Fredrick Nietzsche

WORRY

You cling to my cell membrane
You make me constantly powerless
How the hell am I supposed to cope
When you fire hundreds of thoughts at once
I feel trapped like I'm in a locked maze
Always searching for that exit gate

You think I am quite special
And always cling to me
Letting my dreams slip through my fingers
More and more you make me fall
How the hell am I supposed to reach my destination,
When you don't even let me travel?
You would like to see me doomed, wouldn't you?
The first sign of the storm and I crumble

You would like to see my enemies have more advantage
But I am never going to run like a coward
Even though you make me feel like the victim
And my luck is further away now
And still yet, you creep back
Even when I shut the door

I will still fight even when I am weaker
Laugh your ass off till you fall from the chair
And I will work hard to achieve my goals
And someday I'll laugh at you too

And someday I'll be much wiser
So keep on sneering
Someday I'll be much stronger

"Whoever realises that people are weak in small things, and wants to attain his purpose through them, is always a dangerous human being." Fredrick Nietzsche

THE LITTLE DEVIL
Part 1 (Invader)

From a far distant land
Arrived a devil
They said
He was short
And had intense blue eyes
Mysterious behaviour
Vibes of darkness
The strange smell of a foreigner

His voices were penetrating
And when he spoke
His messages were filled with vision
And his words with courage
To some his speech was alarming
But to his audience
It was crystal clear
Tales of glories

His speech was hypnotising
Seducing like a magician
With it he could lure gullible youths
To jump into fire
His followers grew more and more
The more they listened and cheered
And took oaths of loyalty
Into their heart and souls

His instincts were precise
His fame became notorious
Showed years of mastering the skill
Now he was eager to win the game

When the governor of the town found out
His self-pride and ego let him underestimate
"Fool," laughed wise men
They said, "Let him play for a while."
"Let him have some fun."

In the meantime, little devil carried on
Chanting and poising holy hatred
His aim was to continue the mission
And embed deep enough
For wise men to reach his realisation

The governor did underestimate
Little did he know who he was dealing with
This devil; with precision
And the craft
To carry out the action
Played the illusions; played so well
Underneath the veneer
More soldiers came loyal
He knew how to fool wise men
Until he formed an army of spiteful soldiers
With souls of might
And impenetrable armour

When the governor eventually came to know
Shocked, he was but too little, too late
Too late to realize
That this little devil
Was stronger than they anticipated
Now wise men used all their might to go to the battle field
Now wise men finally began to panic

To combat this devil
They needed to create new ammunitions
They needed to be much stronger
But wise men liked playing with roses
When little devil learned to play with guns
Wise men did not want to dive in dirty water
Beautiful minds in fear

The fierce battle was implemented
I watched hopelessly as days and months passed
And as the chaos followed
Beautiful streets were reduced to squalor
And the victims were beautiful too
Yes it was too little, too late
To bring little devil under restraint

Insane mercenaries, ravaging the streets
And humans dying indiscriminately
People running, people crying;
Societies getting destroyed, hopelessly
The new generation of corrupts were forming
The new age beginning
Fighting for territory
Competing for murder
Amateurs with weapons
Forcing innocent people against their will
Deprivation; lacking humanity
Dancing in the song of terror
Ugly minds germinating foul tricks
They knew how to make profit
Misery was a lucrative business
Beautiful people lost in the colourful sky
Beautiful tongues;
Speechless

Som Gurung

"One pays dearly for being immortal; one dies for it several times during one's life" Fredrick Nietzsche

Part 2 (Challenger)

Me on the other hand, I was still living with wounds
Scarred from the memory of the past
I was locked down in the most dreadful prison
They burned my skin
They caned me with a whooping sound
They treated me like an animal,
Who was unwanted?
And while I cried and screamed
They laughed at my despair

But one day I dared to escape
The dangers of being caught were high
But I said to myself
It's worth the risk that I take
So one day I ran away
And I knew
If I were caught, I would be tortured
Until my death
And that day I decided
To live differently

On the other hand, I was living in nightmares
Fighting every day to keep myself sane
My recollection of that day,
When my legs were bleeding as I ran
And aching tissues, did not make sense
As I ran insanely
My naked feet stumbling; I did not care
I could hear the guards screaming
Senses at alert; crazy dare

42

That day I ran through slopes
I ran through ghettos
Through forests
I was hungry
I was angry
But that did not matter
While I was running out of fear
While I was running to flee horror
I ran like I have never ran before
Because the stakes could never be higher

That day I came across little kids
On the dark avenues
Desperate and filthy
Prowling on the corner
Playing with knives
And I knew what it was like;
I could sympathize
They were suffering with rage too
A new breed trying to alleviate

Created by the part of the system
That ignores the poor and depressed
Where they are only rewarded
If they are violent
And rewarded well they are
Wreckage of poverty
Were called brave in the land deprived

I knew how they were taught
When there is nothing to fear
Others will learn to fear you
But they did not know
When you become fearsome
You will lose everything
And you will live in turmoil everyday
And every day you will be refused
But the lesson I had learned;
No time to share
No time to impart

Som Gurung

The only thing on my mind after running for days
Was still the desperate will to run some more
So that they will never find me
With the full apprehension
And every ounce of energy
Nothing else could I do
I was frightened

As I kept running I passed through stunning lake
By the rays of full moon light
I saw someone in the water drowning
His hands were still fighting
But his head was sinking
Couldn't I have ignored it,
And carried on?
But no! That evening
I went ahead and saved him

He was innocent and charming
Striking looks, but lean
Trembling heavily
Shivering lips, hairy skin
Damp and worn out jeans
Handsome but sad; sad eyes
I said to myself
Just another victim

I was tired
I asked if I could stay the night at his place
The sky was still shining
Birds were asleep; some crickets still screeching
I was gloomy, I was serene
Bitter sweet awareness
In the midst of melancholy; uncanny peace
Finally after walking some distance
We arrived at a little hut, weak and dithering
Inside were two more souls, barely surviving

One of them was a striking lady
Lost in her own world
Tears were still rolling from her eyes

She did not notice this visitor
She did not greet this guest
But just sat by the fire place
Motionless

And the other one was a beautiful little angel
So sound asleep by her mother's side
She looked so peaceful
So gorgeous and so quiet

I looked at her for a while
Then slowly I felt shocked
Then slowly I felt overwhelmed
Then I finally realised fully;
I noticed the pale face
And how cold she was
I screamed inside
Tears were unleashed
Then they started flooding
I did not realised why
Such sweetness; such innocence stolen so early
How could things be in such state of insanity?

He gently lifted the little body into his arms
He held her tightly
Without saying any words I left quietly
Behind me, I heard her weeping
I was left astonished by this way of living;
A new kind of ineptness
There was nothing I could do;
Feeling totally powerless

"The prisoner's wit, which he uses to seek means to free himself by employing each little advantage in the most calculated and exhaustive way, can teach us the tools nature sometimes uses to produce a genius. Nature traps the genius into a prison, and piques to the utmost his desire to free himself" Fredrick Nietzsche

Part 3 (Survivor)

So here I was once again
My city's fate was in the palm of this little devil
A credulous human being; a psychopath
An evil spirit that was destroying
And spoiling the tender hands
And using them to forge a new creation

I acknowledged this was my time;
A time when I have to sacrifice;
To finally confront my past
And I wondered if I would ever be good again;
Be able to leave behind the life of viciousness
I understood that I had to confront
For the sake of beautiful minds
For the sake of friends that I had lost
So I set out to meet him;
This devil worshipper
I made my way to his den;
To meet the one I was waiting for

And the sensation was chilling
Intense feelings
My veneer was firm
But my core was quivering
As I introduced the young soldiers
Bravely staring; new formations
I told them that I have come to serve for their master
I lied about my intention
I was not sure if I would see this devil today
But my fortune finally paid

Stupid Mind

Finally after waiting with patience
Their hero marched forward with mystical gaze
As this little man came closer, everyone showed respect
Looks of amazement; leading them to embrace

Holy Fuck, I looked with astonishment
The clearer I could see; the more I felt at ease
Suddenly I had a bout of weird sensations
Running from my finger tip to my toes
I held my legs tenaciously
I started to feel intensely
I still remember him so vividly
No! Not a bit has he changed

I knew him very well
And if I should talk about him now I should say
Once upon a time
Best player in the game
Found in a gutter, raised in streets
He was dragged through a dirty phase
And grew wiser and older quickly
He mastered all the skills at a tender age
And learned to embrace the game; to uphold it
As a child he too hungered and grieved
But soon enough he swallowed his tears

As he grew older
He became more powerful
And earned more fame;
Pimps, prostitutes, and thugs they all knew his name
He wrote his name in red, he chose his destiny
And followed after him; days of glory

One night all gathered by the fire and followed the ritual
The leaders looked into the sky and with arms wide chanted
vigorously:
*BY THE POWER INVESTED IN ME, I PRONOUNCE YOU
THE CHILD OF THE DEVIL
NOT ONLY WILL YOU BECOME FAMOUS, YOU WILL
MAKE HISTORY
EVEN YOUR ENEMIES WILL START TO TREASURE YOU*

Som Gurung

EVEN THOSE WHO ARE FURIOUS WILL TRUST YOU AND SOMEDAY THEY ALL WILL FOLLOW PASSIONATELY

After that they rejoiced for the whole night
The young and old celebrated together
And exulted the world that thrived on animosity
Preachers of the devil; for sure they knew how to practise it

This one baptised that night was regarded more closely
After all they believed that he would take it beyond
And his steps would keep on leaping
Until the day he would finally rest in peace
So they taught him how to endure
They taught him all the rules of the angry world
But I wonder sometimes
Victims are not always the ones who are crying
Victims are the angry ones too
And the truth is not always what you see
But the truth is also the one that is hiding
Alongside the grimness and the suffering
Everyone needs a silver lining

And I heard he too went in that horrid prison
He too was locked inside
He too was beaten to a pulp
By those cruel and heartless guards
Inside those tormenting walls
With old and fresh blood and other vile smells
Where they say they kept the most disturbed criminals
They said it was where those people belonged
Who were dangerous to society
And even the severest of casualties
Were turned away from sympathy

But unlike others he was thriving inside those walls
He found home amongst those prisoners
Made it a practise ground
There he chastised his wildest temptations

While some went insane completely
While some died inhumanely
He became the one
Whom all the other crooks hailed with admiration
He practised what he preached
He was their new obsession

He shocked everyone;
He started a rebellion
And succeeded in escaping those walls
With a wave of fear
Those notorious guards
Gave in to his rage
The rest of the crooks followed with proud devotion
As he left to carry out his mission
And even his masters cried in admiration
To believe that he was the one

Som Gurung

*"War is the sleep or winter time of culture: man emerges
from it with more strength, both for the good and for the bad"*
Fredrick Nietzsche

Part 4 (Encounter)

So many years had passed since I saw him
But there he was again, pure evil from head to toe
A forceful leader
Powerful and intelligent
As I looked into his eyes
Floating sun sinking in horizon

As he saw me standing he stopped
He looked at me and paused
I couldn't tell if he was surprised or shocked
I was pale
But I still haven't forgotten those days
I stood bravely
And I heard a whisper in my head
A fleeting thought that said
"We will always be associates."

He looked at me in disbelief
Then he spoke to me in excitement
"I cannot believe this is real." His voice was warm
He said he was so pleased to see me again
But I was torn
The dilemma
Should I destroy him regardless?
Now that I can easily win his trust
But he used to be somebody
Who I always wanted to protect
Someone that I never thought I could hurt
When he grinned I felt nostalgia
And a joy to meet with this old friend
But as we embraced
This smile was gone from my face

I stayed the night at his den
I had the whole night to think
What about those beautiful victims;
Would I abandon them?
What about those fighters,
Staring at me in curiosity;
How can I do this?
The eyes of new admirers
The hospitality
The generosity of my host
Trying to lure

When I met him in the morning
Sipping whisky; vintage memo
I looked at him
Delighted with success
I could surely tell
He was far more passionate
He glanced and said
"Rumour had it that you were dead"

I said:
I had been dead for a long time,
And what difference did it make?
But now I exist in a different way;
I live in a different world too
I have changed, my friend
I have changed

I knew I was taking the biggest risk
But I was left with no option
There was no easy way
I had to challenge him that day

So again I spoke:
This is not easy, but I came here to say
That this is now my city
We used to live in peace and harmony
Until you came
And changed everything
So I came to stop you
And I would have succeeded

If we hadn't been friends some day
But now I have failed
I could not have done this to another victim
Even if I wanted

I know those days, it only got worse
When we shivered in the cold
But we also shared our laughter
You will always be that person
You are not the one that I am looking for now

He was not so surprised, but he stared

And in a deep voice he said:
We will keep mourning my friend
We will keep dying
I am guilty of the lives crushed
No regrets: This, my friend is called surviving
When you have nothing
When you are used to being unwanted

Along with the time, paranoia increased
And we never found salvation
But I am here now
As a friend or as an enemy

Remember those times we used to crack jokes
When we used to laugh
It never lasted long
Soon we had to watch each other's back
And redeem from life
What we wanted

He smiled.

My friend
You know that I cannot hurt you either
Even though I have become habitual
But I have come too far
I cannot go back any more

Stupid Mind

Things have changed for the worse since you departed
Now I am creator of something different
And we must follow this tradition
Because this is our only destination

I was not convinced.

I hope someday you can find a reason
To go against the path of destruction
Against all the odds
You can find salvation
In the midst of confusion
You can learn to love
Despite all your vanity
You find peace and serenity
I hope you will someday meet those great nobles
Who still exists
In the heart of this selfishness
As I have changed myself
I hope you too can learn to think differently
With this I give you a little bit of hope
And a little bit of kindness
As I was given
By those great wise men
When I did not think I needed it

I left him feeling contented
But I am glad I have found my reason to live
I raise my hand in solidarity
With the preacher of noble intention

Som Gurung

"Though no stones hear and none can see us each sobs softly, 'remember me. Remember me." Irvin Yalom

Part 5 (Admirer)

One day news passed by
That the little devil was no more
He was shredded in bullet holes
His flesh scattered all over the floor

Born and raised in hell
It came as no surprise at all how he left
It was his final destination
Through hunger and poverty
He saw clearly what was coming from miles away
But he still knew that was what he wanted
Instead of anguish
He chose the way of fatal fame
So much to envy
So much for being born in a poor city

Growing up is not easy
When everything is chaos
Surrounded by troubled people
Learning absurdity in tender age
No aims, no aspirations
So much to figure out with that little brain

And to be haunted by those unrealistic,
Wild and thrilling fantasies
Dreams in ghettos are fatal;
A different form of craziness

Money, fame, sex, parcels in boxes
Running with wolves and sly foxes
What about the reasons he went so far away
What was all that for
He was locked in so many times;

Prisons, hospitals and now his rugged coffin
It is no surprise that mourners are still vigorous
So much for the final day

And in this special day I remembered his words:

I do not want to be remembered after I die
I do not want anyone to lament

So after his funeral, when his body was cremated
His ashes were carried far
And distant
Within a deep forest
They were scattered
Where no hands have ever marred
Where no feet will ever land

"Fine with one another silent
Finer, with one another laughing
Under heaven's silk cloth
Leaning over books and moss
With friends lightly, loudly laughing
Each one showing white teeth shining

If I did well, let us be silent
If I did badly, let us laugh
And do it bad, again by half
More badly done, more badly laugh
Until the grave when down we climb.
Friends! Well what do you say?
Amen! Until we meet again "   .....   Fredrick Nietzsche

www.ingramcontent.com/pod-product-compliance
Lightning Source LLC
Chambersburg PA
CBHW031220290326
41931CB00035B/644